Contents

Introduction

Are you thinking about buying a PV system for your home or business? If so, this booklet will provide basic information that you need to know. Consumers in Pennsylvania, Virginia, Delaware, Maryland, the District of Columbia, West Virginia, and New Jersey are showing increased interest in solar electric systems for their homes and businesses. Photovoltaic (PV) systems are reliable, pollution free, and use a renewable source of energy—the sun. Although they are still expensive, they are becoming more affordable all the time.

Aside from the excellent technological advances and cost reductions in PV technology, several state and federal PV programs and incentives are available to Mid-Atlantic region customers that are making PV systems more economical than ever before. For example, several state government offices offer financial assistance in the form of grants and tax credits to prospective PV customers.

The availability of net metering across the region is also providing an environment more conducive to the provision of cost-effective PV and renewable energy development. Net metering means that when your PV system generates more power than you need, the meter runs backwards, resulting in an even swap for the grid power that you use at other times. In essence, you receive full retail value for all the power that your PV system generates.

This booklet is designed to guide you through the process of buying a solar electric system. A word of caution: this is not a technical guide for designing or installing your system; for that information, we recommend that you consult an experienced PV system designer or system supplier ("PV provider") who will have detailed technical specifications and other necessary information. A PV system can be a substantial investment, and as with any investment, careful planning will help ensure that you make the right decisions.

These materials also provide information on PV programs, incentives, and policies for the states across the region. As the guide evolves, updated and more detailed information on state PV programs and policies will be provided.

What is a solar electric, or photovoltaic, system?

PV technology converts sunlight directly into electricity. It works any time the sun is shining, but more electricity will be produced on sunny days when the light is more intense and is striking the PV modules directly (when the rays of sunlight are perpendicular to the PV modules). Unlike solar systems for heating water, which you might be more familiar with, PV technology does not use the sun's heat to make electricity. Instead, PV produces electricity directly from the electrons freed by the interaction of sunlight with semiconductor materials in the PV cells.

But you don't need to understand the detailed physics of how PV works to understand its appeal: investing in PV allows you to produce your own electricity with no noise, no air pollution, and no moving parts while using a clean, renewable resource. A PV system will never run out of fuel, and it won't increase our oil imports from overseas. In fact, PV may help to reduce the trade deficit because many PV system components are manufactured in the United States. Because of these unique characteristics, PV technology has been called "the ultimate energy source for the 21st century."

The basic building block of PV technology is the solar "cell." PV cells are wired together to produce a PV "module," the smallest component sold commercially, and these modules range in power output from about 10 watts to 300 watts. A PV system tied to the utility grid consists of one or more PV modules connected to an inverter that changes the system's direct-current (DC) electricity to alternating current (AC), which is compatible with the utility grid and able to power devices such as lights, appliances, computers, and televisions. Batteries may be added to the system to provide back-up power in case your utility experiences a power outage.

Some things you should know before purchasing a PV system

First, it produces power intermittently because it works only when the sun is shining. This is not a problem for PV

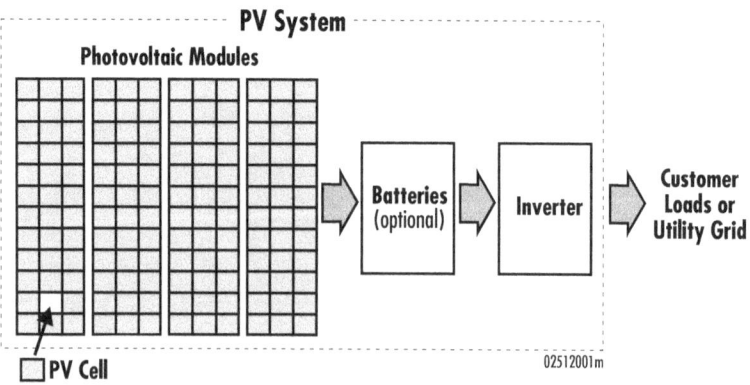

PV System

Photovoltaic Modules

Batteries (optional) → Inverter → Customer Loads or Utility Grid

☐ PV Cell

02512001m

systems connected to the utility grid, because additional electricity you need is automatically delivered to you by your utility.

Second, PV-generated electricity can be more expensive than conventional utility-supplied electricity. Improved manufacturing techniques have reduced the cost to less than 1% of what it was in the 1970s, but the cost (amortized over the life of the system) can be 2-3 times higher than the kilowatt-hour (kWh) rate charged by the utilities in the Mid-Atlantic region. Net metering, which allows residents to spin their electric meters backwards and offset retail electricity costs, can help make PV more affordable, and various incentives can make it cost-effective.

Finally, unlike electricity purchased month by month from a utility, PV power comes with a high initial investment and no monthly charge thereafter. This means that buying a PV system is like paying years of electric bills up-front. You'll probably appreciate the reduction in your monthly electric bills, but the initial expense may be significant. By financing your PV system, you can spread the cost over many years, and state "buy down" grants and other financial incentives can help make the cost more manageable.

A 800-watt solar system being installed on a rooftop will provide about 1/4 the electricity needed by a typical household in the Mid-Atlantic region. If the home is built very efficiently with good exposure to sunlight, the system could supply up to 1/2 of the home's energy needs.

Why should I buy a PV system?

People decide to buy PV systems for a variety of reasons. Some want to help preserve the earth's finite fossil-fuel resources and reduce air pollution. Others believe that it makes more sense to spend their money on an energy-producing improvement to their property than to send their money to a utility. Some people like the security of reducing the amount of electricity they buy from their utility because it makes them less vulnerable to future increases in the price of electricity. Finally, some people just don't like paying utility bills and appreciate the independence that a PV system provides.

Whatever your reason, solar energy is widely thought to be the energy source of choice for the future, and electricity consumers in the Mid-Atlantic region have a unique opportunity to take advantage of state and federally-sponsored programs to help make it their energy choice for today as well as tomorrow.

Is my home or business a good place for a solar system?

Can you orient your system for good performance?

A well-designed PV system needs clear and unobstructed access to the sun's rays for most or all of the day, throughout the year. You can make an initial assessment yourself and, if the location looks promising, your PV provider has the tools to trace the sun's path at your location and determine whether your home or business can make use of a PV solar system.

The orientation of your PV system (the compass direction that your system faces) will affect performance. In the Mid-Atlantic region, the sun is always in the southern half of the sky and is higher in the summer and lower in the winter. Usually, the best location for a PV system is a south-facing roof, but roofs that face east or west may also be acceptable. Flat roofs also work well for solar systems because the PV modules can be mounted flat on the roof facing the sky or mounted on frames tilted toward the south at the optimal angle. If a rooftop can't be used, your solar modules can also be placed on the ground to provide maximum performance.

Is your site free from shading by trees, nearby buildings, or other obstructions?

To make the best use of your PV system, the PV modules must have a clear "view" of the sun for most or all of the day—unobstructed by trees, roof gables, chimneys, buildings, and other features of your home and the surrounding landscape. It is important to note that even though the area where a system is mounted may be unshaded during one part of the day, it may be shaded during another. If this is the case, then this shading may substantially reduce the amount of electricity that your system will produce.

Do you have enough area on your roof or property?

The amount of space needed by a PV system is based on the physical size of the system you purchase. Most residential systems require as little as 50 square feet (for a small "starter" system) up to as much as 1,000 square feet. A typical 1-kilowatt (kW) system would occupy from 80 to 300 square feet, depending on the type and efficiency of modules employed. The table below displays typical roof-area requirements for a range of PV system sizes and module efficiency figures. Although the efficiency (or percent of sunlight converted to electricity) varies with the different types of PV modules available today, higher-efficiency modules generally cost more. Therefore, to meet your long-term energy savings goal, both the cost and the efficiency must be taken into consideration when purchasing a PV system.

What kind of roof do you have, and what is its condition?

Some roof types are simpler and cheaper to work with, but a PV system can be installed on any type. Typically, composition shingles are easiest to work with and slate is the most difficult. In any case, an experienced solar installer will know how to work on all roof types and can use roofing techniques that eliminate any possibility of leaks. Ask your PV provider how the PV system affects your roof warranty.

If your roof is older and needs to be replaced in the very near future, you may want to replace it at the time the PV system is installed to avoid the cost of removing and reinstalling your PV system. Panels often can be integrated into the roof itself, and some modules are actually designed as three-tab shingles or raised-seam metal roof sections. One benefit of these systems is their ability to offset the cost of roof materials.

How big should my PV system be, and what features should it have?

As a starting point, you might consider how much of your present electricity needs you would like to meet with your PV system. For example, suppose that you would like to meet 50 % of your electricity needs with your PV system. You could work with your PV provider to examine past electric bills and determine the size of the PV system needed to achieve that goal.

You can contact your utility and request the total electricity usage, measured in kilowatt-hours, for your household or business over the last 12 months (or consult your electric bills, if you save them). Ask your PV provider how much your new PV system will produce on an annual basis (also measured in kilowatt-hours) and compare that number to your annual electricity demand to get an idea of how much you will save.

Roof Area Needed in Square Feet (shown in **Bold Type**)

PV module efficiency* (%)	PV capacity rating (watts)							
	100	250	500	1,000	2,000	4,000	10,000	100,000
4	30	75	150	300	600	1,200	3,000	30,000
8	15	38	75	150	300	600	1,500	15,000
12	10	25	50	100	200	400	1,000	10,000
16	8	20	40	80	160	320	800	8,000

* Although the efficiency (percent of sunlight converted to electricity) varies with the different types of PV modules available today, higher-efficiency modules typically cost more. So, a less-efficient system is not necessarily less cost-effective.

As you size your system, you should consider the "economies of scale" that can decrease the cost per kilowatt-hour as you increase the size of the system. For example, many inverters are sized for systems up to 5 kW, and if your PV array is smaller (say 3 kW), you may still end up buying the same inverter. Labor costs for a small system may be nearly as much as those for a large system. Therefore, it's worth remembering that your PV provider is likely to offer you a better price to install a 2-kW system all at once, than to install a 1-kW system this year and another next year—multiple orders and multiple site visits are more expensive.

Also, it is generally not economical to try to produce more power than you need. This is because in some states the utility is either not required to compensate the consumer for excess generation above the net metering period or is only required to do so at buyback rates that are low. Typically, this is the utility's "avoided cost" rate that may be a mere fraction, say 20%, of the retail rate provided under net metering.

How much will my PV system save me?

The value of your PV system's electricity will depend on how much you pay your utility for electricity and how much your utility will pay you for any excess that you generate. Because many Mid-Atlantic utilities are required to offer net metering (and provide the full retail credit for your generated, or net excess, electricity), your calculation is fairly easy because you and your utility will each pay the same price for each other's electricity.

A 1-kW system should meet about 12%–18% of the typical residential customer needs. Given the amount of solar resource available in the Mid-Atlantic region, it would produce about 1,600 kWh annually under ideal conditions (i.e., a south-facing installation and proper slope of the roof). If you multiply this annual power output by your average electricity rate (8 cents per kWh or so) and then divide by 12, you come up with a monthly energy savings of about $11 per month. Depending on the grants and incentives involved, a customer should expect to see a system payback of less than 20 years—when the value of energy produced equals the initial investment of the system. This is an achievable goal given the state and local programs and incentives available across the region.

How much does a PV system cost?

There is no single answer, but keep in mind that a solar rebate and other incentives may reduce the cost. Your system's price will depend on a number of factors, including whether the home is under construction or whether the PV is integrated into the roof or mounted on top of an existing roof. The price also varies depending on the PV system rating, manufacturer, retailer, and installer.

The *size* of your system may be the most significant factor in any equation measuring your costs against your benefits. Small, single PV-panel systems with built-in inverters that produce about 75 watts may cost around $900 installed, or $12 per watt. These small systems will offset only a small fraction of your electricity bill. A 2-kilowatt system that will offset the needs of a very energy-efficient home may cost $16,000 to $20,000 installed, or $8 to $10 per watt. At the high end, a 5-kW system that will completely offset the energy needs of many conventional homes may cost $30,000 to $40,000 installed, or $6 to $8 per watt. These prices, of course, are just rough estimates, and your costs will depend on your system's configuration, your equipment options, and other factors. Your local PV providers can provide you with estimates or bids.

Are incentives available to help reduce the cost?

There are numerous state programs and incentives available to help "buy down" the cost of a residential PV system or make it easier to finance. These incentives may include: tax credits, state grants, and low-interest financing packages. Please see the final section of this pamphlet ("State PV Programs, Incentives, and Contacts in the Mid-Atlantic Region") for the most up-to-date information on incentives and financing options for PV systems in your state.

If your home is used for a business, you may be entitled to a 10% federal tax credit and accelerated depreciation on the PV system. These tax benefits can substantially reduce the effective cost of your PV system and should be thoroughly investigated.

How can I finance the cost of my PV system?

There is nothing magical about financing the cost of purchasing and installing your PV system. Although there are some special programs available for financing solar and other renewable-energy investments, most of the options will be familiar to you.

One of the best ways to finance PV systems for homes is through a mortgage loan. Mortgage financing options include your primary mortgage, a second mortgage such as a U.S. Department of Housing and Urban Development (HUD) Title 1 loan, or a home-equity loan that is secured by your property. There are two advantages to mortgage financing. First, mortgage financing usually provides longer terms and lower interest rates than other loans, such as conventional bank loans. Second, the interest paid on a mortgage loan is generally deductible on your federal taxes (subject to certain conditions). If you buy the PV system at the same time that you build, buy, or refinance the house on which the PV system will be installed, adding the cost of the PV system to your mortgage loan is likely to be relatively simple and may avoid additional loan application forms or fees.

If mortgage financing is not available, look for other sources of financing, such as conventional bank loans. Remember to look for the best possible combination of low rate and long term. This will allow you to amortize your PV system as inexpensively as possible. Because your PV system is a long-term investment, the terms and conditions of your PV financing are likely to be the most important factor in determining the effective price of your PV-generated power.

Who sells and installs PV systems?

It will be necessary for consumers to select a vendor to perform the installation of their PV system. We recommend that the prospective customer contact the local chapter of the Solar Energy Industries Association to get help in selecting a contractor/installer (i.e., New York SEIA, Mid-Atlantic SEIA, and Maryland-D.C.-Virginia SEIA.)

In some states with PV grant programs, residents are allowed to select any PV installer they wish. In others, the state government has already selected a qualified contractor through a competitive bid process. You should check with the local Regional Office (RO) of DOE or your state energy office contact listed in the final section of this report. The Philadelphia RO serves the Mid-Atlantic region. The Boston RO serves the New York region and Northeast.

In some locations, finding a PV provider can be as simple as picking up the telephone directory and looking under "Solar Energy Equipment and Systems—Dealers." Be aware, however, that many of those listings are for solar water-heating companies. Many of these companies may not be experienced in PV system design or installation. Similarly, many electrical contractors, although proficient in typical electrical contracting work, may not have expertise in PV or with residential roof-mounting techniques.

How do I choose among PV providers?

Compile a list of prospective PV providers. You might first consider those closest to you, because the contractor's travel costs might add to your

system price. Next, contact these providers and find out what products and services they offer. The following questions may give you a good sense of their capabilities:

Has the company installed grid-connected PV systems? If not, has it installed grid-independent PV systems?

Experience installing grid-connected systems is valuable because some elements of the installation—particularly interconnection with the local utility— are unique to these systems. Because grid-connected systems are relatively uncommon, most contractors with PV experience have worked only on systems such as those that power remote cabins far from the nearest utility line. This means they have experience with all aspects of PV system installation *except* the connection with the utility grid. Although grid-connection work is different from "off-grid" work, a competent company with PV experience should not be eliminated just because it has not installed grid-connected PV systems in the past. In fact, experience with off-grid systems is valuable because grid-independent systems are more technically complicated than grid-tied systems.

How many years of experience does the company have installing PV systems?

This issue speaks for itself: A company or contractor that has been in business a long time has demonstrated an ability to work with customers and to compete effectively with other firms.

Is the company properly licensed?

PV systems should be installed by an appropriately licensed contractor. This usually means that either the installer or

8

a subcontractor has an electrical contractor's license. You must contact the appropriate state agency to verify that a given contractor is licensed to perform the installation. Local building departments also may require that the installer have a general contractor's license. Consumers should call the city and county in which they live for additional information on licensing. Some states even require properly licensed installers to demonstrate that they possess special knowledge about installing PV systems. You should check with your state energy contact. See the list of state energy contacts listed in the final section of this guide.

Does the company have any pending or active judgements or liens against it?

As with any project that requires a contractor, due diligence is recommended. Your State Electrical Board can tell you about any judgments or complaints against a state-licensed electrician. Consumers should call the city and county in which they live for additional information on how to check up on contractors. The Better Business Bureau is another source of information on contractors.

How do I choose among competing bids?

If you have decided to get more than one bid for the installation of your PV system (and it's generally a good idea to do so), you should take steps to ensure that all of the bids you receive are made on the same basis. For example, comparing a bid for a system mounted on the ground against another bid for a rooftop system is like comparing apples to oranges. Similarly, different types of PV modules generate more electricity per square foot than others. Bids should clearly state the maximum generating

capacity of the system (measured in watts or kilowatts). If possible, have the bids specify the system capacity in "AC watts," or specify the output of the system at the inverter.

You may want to obtain some estimate of the amount of energy that the system will produce on an annual basis (measured in kilowatt-hours). Because the amount of energy depends on the amount of sunlight—which varies by location, season, and year to year—it is unrealistic to expect a specific figure. A range of approximately 20% is more realistic. Bids also should include the total cost of getting the PV system up and running, including hardware, installation, connection to the grid, permitting, sales tax, and warranty. Your warranty is a very important factor for evaluating bids. The installer may offer longer warranties. Also ask yourself, "Will this company stand behind the full-system warranty for the next two years?"

Is the lowest price the "best deal"?

It might not be. Often, you get what you pay for. Remember that a PV company is a business just like any other, with overhead and operating expenses that must be covered. It's always possible that a low price could be a sign of inexperience. Companies that plan to stay in business must charge enough for their products and services to cover their costs, plus a fair profit margin. Therefore, price should not be your only consideration.

Remember, if your state has an incentive program for solar energy, it may be through a pre-selected group of contractors. If so, you can only get the incentive by using one of those contractors. Furthermore, most state programs require the prospective PV customer to first contact the state to apply to the grant program and verify that incentives are still available. A customer should not expect to receive incentives or grants after they have installed a system on their own. It is important to contact the state first before proceeding with your solar project.

When the first summer storm knocks out the grid in 1998, "we'll still have power," says Brook. "I think that will be a good time for a party."

What about permits?

If you live in a community in which a homeowners association requires approval for a solar system, you or your PV provider may need to submit your plans. Gain approval from your homeowners association before you begin installing your PV system.

Most likely, you will need to obtain permits from your city or county building department. You will probably need a building permit, an electrical permit, or both before installing a PV system. Typically, your PV provider will take care of this, rolling the price of the permits into the overall system price. However, in some cases, your PV provider may not know how much time or money will be involved in "pulling" a permit. If so, this task may be priced on a time-and-materials basis, particularly if additional drawings or calculations must be provided to the permitting agency. In any case, make sure the permitting costs and responsibilities are addressed at the start with your PV provider.

Code requirements for PV systems vary somewhat from one jurisdiction to the next, but most requirements are based on the National Electrical Code (NEC). The NEC has a special section, Article 690, that carefully spells out requirements for designing and installing safe, reliable, code-compliant PV systems. Because most local requirements are based on the NEC, your building inspector is likely to rely on Article 690 for guidance in determining whether your PV system has been properly designed and installed. If you are among the first people in your community to install a grid-connected PV system, your local building department may not have approved one of these systems. If this is the case, you and your PV provider can speed the process by working closely and cooperatively with your local building officials to help educate them about the technology and its characteristics.

What about insurance?

If you are buying a PV system for your home, your standard homeowner's insurance policy is usually adequate to meet the utility's requirements. However, you may wish to contact your insurance carrier or one of the groups listed in the final section of this booklet. In some states, the electric utility may require additional insurance.

How does the PV system interface with my existing utility connection? What are my options?

There are basically three ways that PV systems can be wired for residential homes: grid-connected, grid connected with battery storage, and off-grid.

Grid-connected implies that the PV system interfaces directly with your current utility connection. This set-up allows the consumer generator to put excess generation (when PV generation exceeds current consumption) back on the grid. In times when consumption exceeds generation by the PV system, the consumer simply obtains the additional power from the local utility as always. Grid-connected systems are gaining in popularity because they do not require battery storage and are more efficient in converting solar energy to electricity. Provided the utility allows net metering, grid-connected systems also tend to be the most cost effective. Under net metering, customers receive full credit for excess electricity from their PV systems at the same rate they normally pay from their utility. In essence, your electric meter will run backward when you are not using all the power that your PV system generates. This topic will be addressed in more detail below in the section on net metering. Several Mid-Atlantic states offer net metering, although the terms and conditions vary in each case.

A second option is *grid-connected with battery storage*. The included battery system provides back-up power in case of a utility power outage. Batteries add value to your system, but at an increased price.

A third option is to operate the PV system *independent of the utility grid*, in cases where the home has no electric service to begin with, or to provide power to outbuildings on a residential property, for example. In cases where a house is off the grid and there are no utility lines available, PV often becomes the most economical choice for both the consumer and the utility. The cost of running a special line is usually more than the cost of installing a PV system.

What about net metering?

Net metering has been generally accepted as one of the best, unobtrusive ways for states to encourage consumers to purchase renewable energy systems. Basically, net metering allows customers to only pay for their "net" electricity or the amount of power consumed from the utility minus the power generated at the customer's home via the PV system. Excess generation (power not consumed during the billing period) may be met with a reimbursement at the utility's avoided cost (usually a much lower rate) or not at all.

Once the utility has been contacted and has cleared your PV system for net metering, you should check that you are receiving credit. On a bright sunny day, when few or no lights or appliances in your house are running, examine your electric meter. You should observe it spinning in reverse. You should note the meter reading, then check again in a few hours and see if the meter reading is lower. In most circumstances, the "old fashioned" meter with mechanical dials works fine. However, some newer electronic meters have trouble registering electricity flow in reverse. Your PV installer should be able to let you know if you will have a problem.

What about utility and inspection sign-off?

After your new PV system is installed, it may need to be inspected and "signed off" by the local permitting agency (usually a building or electrical inspector) and perhaps by the electric utility. Inspectors may require your PV provider to make corrections, but don't be alarmed, this is fairly common in the construction business.

What about warranties?

Warranties are key to ensuring that your PV system will be repaired if something should malfunction during the warranty period. PV systems should carry a full (not "limited") two-year warranty, in addition to any manufacturers' warranties on specific components. This warranty should cover all parts and labor, including the cost of removing any defective component, shipping it to the manufacturer, and reinstalling the component after it is repaired or replaced.

Be sure you know who is responsible for honoring the various warranties associated with your system—the installer, the dealer, or the manufacturer. The vendor should disclose the warranty responsibility of each party. Know the financial arrangements, such as contractor's bonds, that assure the warranty will be honored. Remember, a warranty does not guarantee that the company will remain in business. Get a clear understanding of whom you should contact if there is a problem. To avoid any later misunderstandings, be sure to read the warranty carefully and review the terms and conditions with your retailer.

Appendix
National, Regional, and State PV Programs, Incentives, and Contacts

The Utility Photovoltaic Group and the TEAM-UP Initiative

The UPVG

The Utility Photovoltaic Group (UPVG) is a nonprofit association of nearly 100 energy service providers (electric utilities and energy service companies) dedicated to accelerating the use of photovoltaics for the benefit of electric utilities and their customers so that photovoltaics become a sustainable energy option and a thriving domestic industry. The UPVG, with funding support from DOE, is led and managed by the market itself—the potential utility buyers of solar photovoltaic systems. The UPVG programs are increasing the experience of electric utilities and their customers with photovoltaics and are stimulating growth in the demand for solar power. The UPVG maintains a comprehensive Web site at *www.upvg.org*

The UPVG program recognizes that many utilities lack knowledge or are skeptical about the potential of PV systems. For the market to proceed to widespread commercial applications, utilities need to gain greater confidence in the technology's role. Created in September of 1992, the UPVG now is concentrating on educating utility and other audiences and is helping to build a foundation for utility PV purchase commitments through its DOE-sponsored *TEAM-UP* initiative.

The TEAM-UP Initiative

The *TEAM-UP* initiative (Technology Experience to Accelerate Markets for Utility Photovoltaics) is a utility-government partnership program to co-fund the deployment of demonstration and field validation photovoltaic (PV) systems. *TEAM-UP*'s goal is to develop a market to help the PV industry move closer to the point of domestic commercial sustainability. In all, six rounds of *TEAM-UP* procurements have been scheduled to complete implementation of the *TEAM-UP* initiative, where the industry is investing nearly four dollars for every dollar invested by the U.S. taxpayer.

Since 1995, the UPVG, funded in part by DOE, has managed the *TEAM-UP* initiative. *TEAM-UP* has funded 36 business ventures through three rounds of competitively selected awards, representing 130 partners in 30 states. These projects are expected to significantly increase the experience of electric utilities and their customers with photovoltaics and will stimulate growth in the demand for solar power across the nation. To date, *TEAM-UP* has awarded $15 million in DOE funds for programs to invest in PV business ventures in the United States. This will result in more than 2,500 PV installations in as many as 30 states with the involvement of 47 energy service providers. This $15 million from DOE funding has leveraged over $57 million in investments from private industry for a total of $72 million of new PV installations. These new PV system installations, totaling more than 7.5 megawatts of power, will stimulate markets that will reduce the cost and increase the deployment of PV systems, leading to more American jobs and a cleaner environment. These ventures have the potential to create tens of millions of dollars of new investment in the domestic use of solar electric power.

The Future

The UPVG program has been very successful and is continuing the very important education and outreach activities. The *TEAM-UP* program is just now hitting stride, with almost 3.5 MW of PV systems installed and another 4.0 MW in the pipeline for deployment in the next two years. These "mainstream" installations will create a strong impetus for long-term domestic investment in PV technology, and maintain the United States as the world leader in this energy technology. This program needs to continue and complete the six rounds to stimulate a self-sustaining and strong domestic market for U.S. PV products.

Based on the first three rounds, the UPVG's *TEAM-UP* initiative is strong evidence of the electric industry's commitment to new and environmentally clean technologies. The program demonstrates how effective a partnership between the government and private industry can be where the government supplies incentive, private industry shoulders most of the cost, and the nature of the investments is determined by the marketplace.

Much of this new investment will be for community-based solar installations. *TEAM-UP* is building on what UPVG members are already doing—responding to customer demand for solar and other renewables and developing a commercial market for PV. Extensive market research has indicated that customers are willing to pay a premium for "green electricity," and many of the *TEAM-UP* ventures have incorporated green-pricing programs where customers are willing to pay more on their utility bill for clean energy. Aided by UPVG and *TEAM-UP*, electric utilities can greatly expand the opportunity for customers to choose solar electricity in their homes and businesses.

TEAM-UP Funding

The funding by DOE for the *TEAM-UP* initiative is as follows:

TEAM-UP Round	DOE Funding Share	Private Cost
Round One	$4,300,000	$17,500,000
Round Two	$5,800,000	$17,800,000
Round Three	$5,000,000	$22,500,000
Round Four	???	???
Total	$15,100,000	$57,800,000

For more information on *TEAM-UP*, please contact the UPVG at 202-857-0898 or via the Internet at *www.ttcorp.com/upvg*

Mid-Atlantic Regional PV Programs, Incentives, and Contacts

Virginia Alliance for Solar Electricity (VASE)

The Virginia Alliance for Solar Electricity (VASE) is a partnership that began with Solarex, Virginia Power, Virginia's Center for Innovative Technology (CIT), the Virginia Department of Mines, Minerals and Energy (DMME), and DOE to accelerate the commercialization of a new generation of photovoltaic (PV) modules manufactured in Virginia by Solarex. The VASE partnership has expanded from its original partners and now includes other states in the Mid-Atlantic region, including New Jersey, Pennsylvania, Maryland, and North Carolina.

The VASE program was awarded cost-share funding from DOE under the Commercialization Ventures Program through a cooperative agreement made to DMME. This cost-share funding is being used to "buy down" the cost of Solarex's new tandem-junction amorphous silicon thin-film photovoltaic modules manufactured at their Virginia plant. The VASE partners are identifying eligible building owners and developers interested in installing this PV technology. For more information about the VASE partnership, VASE-funded projects, and technology applications, please visit the VASE Web site (*www.vase.org*). The VASE contact person at Solarex is Chris Whiteley 301-698-4275.

For more information about Solarex, their products, and manufacturing facilities, please visit the Solarex Web site (*www.solarex.com*).

DOE's Million Solar Roofs' Solar Energy Loan Program

DOE's Federal Credit Union is currently working with Solarex and VASE to develop a "Million Solar Roofs' Solar Energy Loan Program." The program has been awarded funding through the VASE program for 100 kW residential systems and it offers prospective consumers very attractive financing terms, including a 15-year, fixed-rate solar home equity loan with a quarter point of interest reduced.

Term	Annual Percentage Rate (Fixed)	Loan-to-Value
5 years	6.50%	80%
10 years	7.00%	80%
15 years	7.50%	80%

For more information, visit the following Web sites:

DOE Energy Efficiency and Renewable Energy Network—
www.eren.doe.gov/millionroofs

Home Energy Saver Advisor—
www.hes.lbl.gov

State Energy Alternatives MD—
www.eren.doe.gov/state_energy/mystate.cfm?state=MD

State Energy Alternatives VA—
www.eren.doe.gov/state_energy/mystate.cfm?state=VA

U.S. Department of Energy—
www.doe.gov

The Energy Federal Credit Union (EFCU) suggests that customers interested in the Solar Mortgage Loan Program visit the nearest EFCU branch location or call the Member Service Call Center at 301-670-1300 or 800-223-2177 and press 4. The EFCU Web site at *www.energyfcu.org* also contains information on the program.

Townhouses in Bowie, Maryland have standing-seam roofs. One has an integrated PV standing-seam roof that looks and performs like the standard metal roofing on the other units, but it produces electricity. The PV modules closely match the look of the standard metal roofing modules, preserving a consistent, attractive appearance.

State PV Programs, Incentives, and Contacts in the Mid-Atlantic Region

Delaware

State Contact

Suzanne Sebastian
Energy Program Manager
Division of Facilities Management
410 Federal Street, Suite 2
Dover, DE 19901
302-739-5644
302-739-6148
ssebastian@state.de.us (e-mail)

District of Columbia

State Contacts and Other Resources

D.C. Department of Energy
2000 14th Street, NW
Suite 300
Washington, DC 20009
202-673-6738

Maryland, DC, Virginia Solar Energy Industries Association
Steve Kalland, Acting Director
c/o Capital Sun Group
6503 81st Street
Cabin John, MD 20818
301-229-0671
301-229-0289 (fax)

This organization represents the Mid-Atlantic region in the Solar Energy Industries Association, the national trade association of the solar industry. Contact them for information about solar energy and various PV applications.

Maryland

Maryland was the first state in the country to have a functioning solar program in place. The Maryland Solar Roofs Program is comprised of the Residential Rooftop Program, the Solar Schools Program, the Solar for Farms Program, and municipal solar projects. Maryland passed a PV net metering law in 1997, and recently extended net metering to include schools and churches.

Incentives and Programs

Net Metering

In the 1997 session of the Maryland General Assembly, the legislature passed net metering legislation for the use of photovoltaic systems on residences throughout the State. The legislation required all utilities to allow the use of a single meter to register forward and reverse flows of power. To qualify for net metering in Maryland, PV systems must not have a peak generating capacity of more than 80 kW (80,000 watts). Compliant systems must also be UL listed and comply with Article 690 of the National Electric Code and IEEE standards. Systems installed by a contractor under the Residential Rooftops Program assures that the contractor was informed of and met these requirements.

Maryland utilities are required to connect customers who comply with these requirements to the grid and provide net metering service. (Note: the Maryland law limits the total amount of PV that can be "net metered" to 0.2% of the utility peak load or about 34 megawatts statewide.) To learn the exact terms, contact the Maryland Public Service Commission and request a copy of the net metering tariff for your electric utility. Some utilities may require an interconnection agreement and inspection; others may just require notice.

In most circumstances, the "old fashioned" utility meter with mechanical dials works fine under net metering. However, some newer electronic meters have trouble registering electricity flow in reverse. Your PV installer should be able to let you know if you will have a problem. If you are unsure, contact the engineering division of the Maryland Public Service Commission and ask for a test of the meter in **both directions** (forward and reverse).

Maryland Residential Rooftops Program

Overview

The Maryland Residential Rooftops Program, currently in its second year, is a statewide initiative to stimulate the increased use of photovoltaic energy by residential consumers. Sponsored by the Maryland Energy Administration (MEA), the program provides grants to help Maryland electricity consumers purchase solar PV systems. The MEA also simplifies the process required for customers to purchase their systems by selecting a contractor/installer through a competitive procurement process. In so doing, the State can be certain that its grant funds and customers are going to an experienced and qualified contractor. This method also assures that the customers receive the most competitive price and a positive first experience in purchasing a PV system.

The program will continue to increase the number of PV installations each year to reach Maryland's goal of 1/50 of installed systems by 2010 under the Federal Million Solar Roofs Initiative. The Million Roofs Initiative seeks to install one million PV systems nationwide by 2010. Under the first year of the program, 10 systems were successfully installed. During 1999, the MEA will oversee the installation of 20 systems, and this figure will double each of the next 5 years. The program's broader, long-term purpose is to develop a self-sustaining regional market for solar energy. This includes an infrastructure of manufacturers, distributors and installers, and a trained cadre of electricians and builders familiar with the technology.

The grant monies offered by the program will decline each year in response to expected declines in the cost of solar PV systems. During 1998, the grant amount was $4,000 per system, but this will decline to approximately $3,600 per system during 1999, and will be further reduced in subsequent years. The grant monies are incorporated into the system price offered to the consumer by the MEA-selected installer.

Requirements

There are several aspects of the Residential Rooftops that prospective customers must consider:

• Customers who wish to participate in the Residential Rooftops Program and receive the excellent system prices offered through State grants must work with the installer selected by the MEA. Customers that install systems on their own, independent of the program, can not then apply for grant assistance.

• The minimum system size for PV systems installed under the program is 1.2kW. Customers may increase the size of their systems at their discretion, but the State grant amount incorporated into their system price remains constant.

• The customer's home must be located in Maryland.

• The customer must contact the MEA to verify that grant funds are still available.

Jonathan Cross
Maryland Energy Administration
45 Calvert Street
Annapolis, MD 21401
410-260-7184
410-974-2250 (fax)
jcross@energy.state. md.us (e-mail)

Maryland, DC, Virginia Solar Energy Industries Association
Steve Kalland, Acting Director
c/o Capital Sun Group
6503 81st Street
Cabin John, Maryland 20818
301-229-0671
301-229-0289 (fax)

This organization represents the Mid-Atlantic region in the Solar Energy Industries Association, the national trade association of the solar industry. Contact them for information about solar energy and various PV applications.

The Maryland Public Service Commission
William Donald Schaefer Tower
6 St. Paul Street
Baltimore, MD 21202
410 767-8112
410-333-6844 (fax)

The Maryland Public Service Commission regulates the State's utilities. Utility customers have the right to file an informal or formal complaint with the Commission. Individuals, groups, or organizations can also intervene or participate in formal cases before the Commission, and can testify at public hearings that the Commission holds across the state.

New Jersey

Incentives and Programs

New Jersey offers several programs and incentives for solar energy and in-state entities have been very active in installing PV systems on residential and commercial facilities.

Net Metering

New Jersey's legislation, which deregulated electricity supply, requires net metering for both PV and wind energy. The law applies to both residential and small commercial customers for net metered PV systems. Net excess generation is credited the following month and is purchased by the utility at avoided wholesale cost.

Sales Tax Incentive

The technologies that are eligible for this incentive include: passive-solar space heat, active-solar water heat, active-solar space heat, solar-thermal electricity, photovoltaics, wind, biomass, hydro, alternative fuels, and water pumping. It addresses all sectors: industrial, commercial, residential, and all utilities. Basically, New Jersey offers a full exemption from the state 6% sales tax for all solar and wind equipment. This exemption, which was created in 1980 and is scheduled to expire in 2000, is available to all taxpayers. (Courtesy of the North Carolina Solar Center (NCSC), *http://www.ncsc.ncsu.edu/*)

The point of contact for the incentive is Cameron Johnson at the New Jersey Board of Public Utilities, at: 44 South Clinton Avenue Box 350, Trenton, NJ 08625-0350. Her telephone is 609-777-3316 and fax is 609- 777-3336.

Technical Sufficiency Standards for Solar Energy Devices

This is an equipment certification standard for solar generation equipment. Eligible technologies include: passive solar space heat, active solar water heat, active solar space heat, solar industrial process heat and solar thermal activity, in addition to photovoltaics. The program addresses commercial, industrial and residential sectors.

New Jersey's technical sufficiency standards for solar equipment were established to certify eligible solar-energy equipment for the State's sales and use tax exemptions. The statute defines all relevant solar-energy equipment, including equipment for passive-solar design. Acceptable certification standards/organizations include Solar Rating and Certification Corporation (SRCC), Air-Conditioning and Refrigeration Institute (ARI), or American Society of Heating, Refrigeration, and Air-Conditioning Engineers (ASHRAE). The point of contact for more information is also Cameron Johnson. (Courtesy of NCSC)

Sustainable Development Loan Fund

The New Jersey Commerce and Economic Growth Commission, Office of Sustainable Business, offers low-interest loans to New Jersey businesses that wish to install renewable energy systems. The Office of Sustainable Business also provides full funding packages for companies that produce renewable energy technologies within the state of New Jersey.

For more information, call Cassandra Kling at 609-633-3655.

State Contacts

Cameron Johnson
New Jersey Division of Energy
P.O. Box 350
Trenton, NJ 08625-0350
609-777-3316
609-777-3330 (fax)
johnsonc@bpu.state.nj.us (e-mail)

Mid-Atlantic Solar Energy Industries Association
Lyle Rawlings, President
66 Snydertown Rd.
Hopewell, NJ
609-466-4495;609-466-8681

NJ Commerce and Economic Growth Commission
Office of Sustainable Business
Cassandra Kling
28 West State Street
P.O. Box 819
Trenton, NJ 08625-0820

Pennsylvania

Pennsylvania recently began competitive retail electricity service, allowing two-thirds of all customer classes (residential, commercial, and industrial) to have freedom of choice for selecting an electricity generation supplier. They also passed net metering legislation during 1998.

Incentives and Programs
Net Metering

As a result of the restructuring of the electricity industry in the state, some utilities are offering net metering for systems up to 10kW. A utility may or may not pay for any electricity generated in excess of the system owner's own usage. Contact the utility in your area.

State Contacts and Other Resources

James M. McTish, Jr.
Pennsylvania Department of Environmental Protection
Lee Park, Suite 6010
555 North Lane
Conshohocken, PA 19428
610-832-6098
610-832-6133 (fax)
mctish.james@dep.state.pa.us (e-mail)

**Pennsylvania Solar Energy
Industries Association**
(Merging with the new Mid-Atlantic
SEIA this year)
Bob Nape, President
c/o Solar Techniques
5919 Pulaski Avenue
Philadelphia, PA 19144
215-844-4196
215-844-4196 (fax)
Bobnape@aol.com (e-mail)

**Philadelphia Million Solar Roofs
Community Partnership**
Energy Coordinating Agency of
Philadelphia, Inc.
Scott Hunter
1924 Arch Street
Philadelphia, PA 19103
(215) 988-0929
(215) 988-0919 (fax)
scott@ecasavesenergy.org (email)

Virginia

Virginia offers an energy efficiency and renewable energy loan program, tax exemptions, and recently passed net metering legislation. It is also home to the Virginia Alliance for Solar Electricity program, which was recently expanded across the Mid-Atlantic region.

Incentives and Programs

Renewable Energy and Energy Efficiency Loan Program

This residential loan program, which was created under HUD Title 1 in 1978, is administered by the Virginia Housing Development Authority. The program makes low-interest loans available for low and moderate income homeowners for repairs that reduce energy consumption or reduce dependence on conventional energy sources. All renewable energy technologies are eligible, including passive-solar space heat, active-solar water heat, active-solar space heat, solar-thermal electricity, photovoltaics, wind, biomass, hydro, geothermal, and waste. The interest rate is 6.75%. Additionally, there is an annual Federal Housing Association insurance charge of one-half of one percent (0.5%) of the loan amount. Loan amounts range from $1,000 to $25,000 for terms from 6 months up to 20 years. (A lien on the property is required for all loan amounts.) Borrowers can borrow up to 100% of the equity in their home. About 100 loans are made per year. The incentive provides 100% of equity and terms of up to 20 years. The point of contact for the program is Julia Perkinson, Virginia Housing Development Authority, 601 S. Belvidere Street, Richmond, VA 23220-6500. Her phone is 804-782-1986 and fax is (804) 783-6737.

Local Option Property Tax Exemption

This statute allows any county, city or town to exempt, or partially exempt, solar-energy equipment or recycling equipment from local property taxes. Residential, commercial, or industrial property is eligible. The statute broadly defines solar-energy equipment as any "application that would otherwise require a conventional source of energy." Recycling equipment is defined as equipment that is "integral to the recycling process and for use primarily for the purpose of abating or preventing pollution of the atmosphere or waters." It addresses the following technologies: passive-solar space heat, active-solar water heat, active-solar space heat, solar-thermal electricity, and photovoltaics. To determine if the locality that you are in offers this property-tax exemption, contact your local commissioner of revenue and cite the following Section from the Code of Virginia, §58.1-3661.

Net Metering

In March, 1999, the Virginia state legislature enacted legislation (Virginia Assembly bill S1269) requiring net metering for small solar, wind, and hydro-electric systems. The law requires all of the state's utilities to offer net metering to residential systems of 10 kW or less and nonresidential systems of 25 kW or less. The law limits the amount of net metered generation to 0.1% of the previous year's peak electricity demand. Customers can apply the credit for electricity generated from their system to the following month; however, at the end of the year, any excess generation is granted to the utility. The law required the Virginia State Corporation Commission to establish by regulation the net metering program to begin no later than July 1, 2000. For more information on net metering, contact your local utility provider or Mr. Ken Jurman, Virginia Department of Mines, Minerals and Energy, 202 North 9th Street, 8th Floor, Richmond, Virginia 23219, 804-692-3222.

Virginia Solar PV Manufacturing Incentive Grant Program

Virginia offers photovoltaic manufacturing companies who locate their operations in Virginia one of the most far-reaching incentive grants available. The program was designed to create jobs and economic development in Virginia by encouraging the manufacture of a high-tech renewable energy project in Virginia. It provides perfor mance-based incentive grants (up to $0.75/watt) directly to the companies who sell PV modules that they manufacture in Virginia. Since the program was created, Virginia has attracted two PV manufacturing companies, including BP Solarex and Solar Building Systems. For more information on this program, contact: Mr. Ken Jurman, Virginia Department of Mines, Minerals and Energy, 202 North 9th Street, 8th Floor, Richmond, Virginia 23219, 804-692-3222.

State Contacts and Other Resources
Ken Jurman
Division of Energy
The Department of Mines, Minerals and Energy
9th Street Office Building, 8th Floor
202 North 9th Street
Richmond, VA 23219
804-692-3226

Maryland, DC, Virginia Solar Energy Industries Association
Steve Kalland, Acting Director
c/o Capital Sun Group
6503 81st Street
Cabin John, MD 20818
301-229-0671
301-229-0289 (fax)

This organization represents the Mid-Atlantic region in the Solar Energy Industries Association, the national trade association of the solar industry. Contact them for information about solar energy and various PV applications.

West Virginia
State Contact
Bill Willis
West Virginia Development Office
1900 Kanawha Boulevard East
Charleston, WV 25305-0311

www.ingramcontent.com/pod-product-compliance
Lightning Source LLC
Chambersburg PA
CBHW072014280526
45788CB00005B/2042